PREHISTORIC SAFARI
GIANT DINOSAURS

Liz Miles

RiverStream

Hardcover edition first published in 2012 by Arcturus Publishing

Hardcover Library bound edition distributed by Black Rabbit Books
P. O. Box 3263
Mankato
Minnesota MN 56002

Published by arrangement with Arcturus Publishing

Library of Congress Cataloging-in-Publication Data

Miles, Liz.
 Giant dinosaurs / by Liz Miles.
     p. cm. – (Prehistoric safari)
 Includes index.
 ISBN 978-1-84858-568-3 (hardcover, library bound)
 1. Dinosaurs–Juvenile literature. I. Title.
 QE861.5.M5536 2013
 567.9–dc23

                                2011051443

Text: Liz Miles
Editor: Joe Harris
Picture researcher: Joe Harris
Design: Emma Randall
Cover design: Emma Randall

Picture credits:
De Agostini Picture Library: 7tr, 7cr, 9cr, 11br, 13br, 15tr, 19cr, 19br, 21tr, 23cr, 25br,
27tr, 27cr, 27br. Highlights for Children, Inc.: 7br, 15cr, 19tr. iStockphoto: 11tr, 11cr. Miles
Kelly Publishing Ltd: 13cr, 23tr, 23br. Natural History Museum, London: 13tr, 21cr, 21br.
pixel-shack.com: cover (main) 1, 5tr, 6–7, 8–9, 12–13, 14–15, 22–23, 24–25, 25tr, 28t.
Shutterstock: cover (top images) 2–3, 4–5, 5cr, tbr, 10–11, 16–17, 17tr, 17br, 18–19,
20–21, 26–27, 29 (all). Wikimedia: 9tr, 9br, 15br, 17cr, 25cr, 28b

SL002122US

1 2 3 4 5 CG 15 14 13 12
RiverStream Publishing—Corporate Graphics, Mankato, MN—122012—1008CGF12
Paperback version printed in the USA

CONTENTS

GIANT SAFARI

Are you ready for a truly breathtaking adventure? You are about to parachute from a plane down to a secret island—an island full of huge prehistoric monsters. Your goal is to capture the biggest dinosaur of all on film. Your tracking skills, your sprinting ability, and your bravery are going to be essential.

As you fly over the island, a group of flying reptiles swoops dangerously close to your plane. They must be *Pteranodon*.

Soon you will be facing predators with teeth like swords and armored heavyweights like *Triceratops*—which could flatten you underfoot or impale you with its horns.

The pilot circles low, looking for a safe landing site for your parachute jump. You stare from the window, amazed that the island is home to creatures that are meant to have died out 65 million years ago.

SAFARI ESSENTIALS

Gingko leaves Some of the biggest dinosaurs are plant-eaters, so tasty leaves from this tree might prove a useful distraction. Gingkos are called "living fossils," as similar plants existed up to 270 million years ago.

Camera Your friends are unlikely to believe what you see on safari—so you will need lots of photos as proof. A good zoom lens means you won't have to get too close.

dinoPad All the dinosaur facts you need to know have been downloaded onto your electronic reader.

LONG NECKS

The parachute drop is over in seconds. The breeze carries you down onto a wet, sandy beach, right next to a herd of gigantic *Brachiosaurus*. They call to each other—do they see you as a threat? You back away from their powerful tails and quickly gather up the parachute. Then you follow the giants as they amble along the beach, into a forested area.

As high as a ten-story building, a *Brachiosaurus* can stretch its long neck to graze on the topmost leaves of conifer trees. It leaves footprints 40 in (1 m) long.

Its chisel-like teeth are good for cutting but not chewing. To help digest tough leaves, it swallows stones that grind the greens in its giant-sized stomach.

Brachiosaurus is a sauropod. The sauropod group of four-legged dinosaurs includes the largest land animals ever known.

Meaning of name: Arm lizard
Height: 50 ft (15 m)
Length: 100 ft (30 m)
Family: Brachiosauridae
Period: Late Jurassic
Weight: 88 tons (80,000 kg)
Found in: Algeria, Portugal, Tanzania, USA
Diet: Plants

GRAZERS

Many of the biggest dinosaurs are herbivores (plant-eaters).

▼ *Alamosaurus*
In spite of its size, the powerful back legs of the *Alamosaurus* are strong enough to take its full weight when stretching to reach the topmost branches of trees.

▶ *Iguanodon*
The plant-eating *Iguanodon* has tough teeth in its beaklike mouth for grinding up plants.

◀ **Prehistoric plants**
Flowering plants did not become common until the Cretaceous period. Before that, sauropods had to feed on tough-leaved evergreens, such as conifers and cycads.

SPINY HUNTER

You slip cautiously through the sharp-leaved plants to a sunlit swamp, where you come across a huge predator. The creature—a *Spinosaurus*—is peering into a pool of water. Suddenly it snatches up a fish. You see sharp teeth and catch the stench of its foul breath. Then it turns and looks straight at you. Time to make a quick escape!

Unlike other meat-eating dinosaurs, spinosaurids have a long, narrow snout and small, sharp teeth—useful for snapping up slippery fish.

Spinosaurids eat mainly carrion and fish. The big claws on their thumbs are used for defense and to grasp fish.

The "sail" of skin and bone on the *Spinosaurus'* back might be used like a solar panel to help heat up its body and a car radiator to cool it down, or for display.

SAILS AND FINS

▶ *Spinosaurus*
The *Spinosaurus'* "sail" contains spines that stand up from the backbone, up to 6.5 ft (2 m) high.

▼ *Acrocanthosaurus* is a killer with a small fin down its back. This is thicker than *Spinosaur*'s sail and might be used for fat storage or signalling.

▼ *Dimetrodon* The 10 ft- (3 m-) high *Dimetrodon* is the most aggressive predator of the Permian period. It has an impressive sail that must terrify its prey.

Spinosaurus, a theropod, is probably the longest (but not overall biggest) meat-eater to walk the planet.

Meaning of name: Thorn lizard
Height: 17 ft (5 m)
Length: 52 ft (16 m)
Family: Spinosauridae
Period: Late Cretaceous
Weight: 4 tons (3,600 kg)
Found in: Egypt, Morocco
Diet: Meat

MONSTER FOOTPRINTS

You run until you are out of breath, and clear of the trees. There you find a set of prints, which you start to follow. Before long, you discover the source of the trail—a herd of *Diplodocus*. You used to think of these as gentle giants, but now realize their tails are powerful weapons. Something flashes before your eyes! You crouch to avoid another crack of the "whip."

Diplodocus' pencil-sharp teeth, downturned head, and long neck are used to feed on a wide area of low-growing plants. It grazes like a cow.

There are nostrils on the top of its head—useful to sniff the air for likely predators as it grazes.

The head is small compared to the body, with room for just a tiny brain. It is not very intelligent.

Diplodocus is one of the most famous dinosaurs and travels in grazing herds.

Meaning of name: Double beam
Height: 16 ft (5 m)
Length: 90 ft (27 m)
Family: Diplodocidea
Period: Late Jurassic
Weight: 12 tons (11,000 kg)
Found in: United States
Diet: Plants

FEET AND FOOTPRINTS
Fossil footprints show how dinosaurs walked.

◄ *Diplodocus* leaves huge back footprints and smaller front footprints. It walks on thick pads and three toes, built to take the weight of its massive body. The front feet have sharp thumb claws. It walks slowly.

► *Tyrannosaurus* and other meat-eaters leave large, birdlike footprints. They move on two legs, and can run fast. Three of the four toes on each foot touch the ground.

▼ *Triceratops* leave smaller prints than long-necked sauropods, but their depth shows the heavy weight of their bodies. They are slow, plodding walkers.

GIANT EGGS

While crouching, you spot something that looks like a white football. A closer look at the "ball," and you realize it's a huge egg. Then you see another, and another. The last is warm, recently laid. A few more steps and there's the spectacular egg-layer—an *Apatosaurus*, even sturdier looking than a *Diplodocus*. It wanders off, leaving the eggs to hatch alone.

Apatosaurus does not take care of its eggs or its newly hatched young. The eggs are an easy meal for predators.

Apatosaurus lays its eggs as it walks, each egg dropping about 8 ft (2.5 m) onto the ground without breaking.

Apatosaurus eggs are up to 1 ft (30 cm) in diameter.

Apatosaurus (once known as a *Brontosaurus*) is a massive sauropod, but harmless—unless it steps on you.

Meaning of name: Deceptive lizard
Height: 13 ft (4 m)
Length: 70 ft (21 m)
Family: Diplodocidea
Period: Late Jurassic
Weight: 33 tons (30,000 kg)
Found in: United States
Diet: Plants

EGGS AND NESTS

▶ Eggs are a perfect meal for a beaky dinosaur like *Gallimimus*. Its long, toothless jaws can easily crack the shell of a small dinosaur egg.

▼ Most dinosaurs lay their eggs in nests (a mound of soil or mud), like *Maiasaura* (which means "good-mother lizard"). *Maiasaura* may look after their young for years and travel with them in herds.

▼ The biggest dinosaur egg fossils ever found are ellipsoid in shape and 16 in (41 cm) long.

WALKING TANKS

You soon come across four awesome, horned monsters—the tanklike *Triceratops*! These creatures seem to be on edge, so you are relieved to remember they are herbivores. You witness a head-to-head combat between two males. Horns crack and crash. The whole forest shakes as another joins in. It's time to beat a hasty retreat, before you are trampled...

The three sharp horns are used to battle with other males as they fight over mates. They are also useful for fighting off predators. By stabbing the underbellies of dinosaurs like *Tyrannosaurus* they can escape.

The frill protects the vulnerable neck from a deadly bite, tearing claw, or jabbing horn.

Triceratops' teeth are like shears, perfect for chomping through low-growing plants.

Triceratops is a fearsome, three-horned plant-eater.

Meaning of name: Three-horned face
Height: 10 ft (3 m)
Length: 30 ft (9 m)
Family: Ceratopidae
Period: Late Cretaceous
Weight: 6 tons (5,400 kg)
Found in: United States
Diet: Plants

FRILLED FACES

▼ *Chasmosaurus* has a huge, rectangular neck frill. Instead of solid bone, which would have been too heavy, it is made up of bone struts, with skin stretched across.

◀ *Styracosaurus* can form a wall of defense with their 2-ft- (60-cm-) long horns and frills, by gathering in herds. The younger, more vulnerable, *Styracosaurus* are protected by staying near the middle.

▶ *Centrosaurus* has a frill that is too thin for defense. Instead, it may have been for show, to scare off predators, or to attract mates. This skull shows the holes in the frill, which make it lighter.

DRAGON DINOSAUR

You follow a rustling in the trees—and almost run into the mouth of a dragonlike *Ceratosaurus*! You clamber up a conifer tree, but only just in time. You cling tight—one slip and you will be minced by those bladelike teeth. Suddenly the predator swings its head away, spots some easier prey, and strides away.

The horns and jagged crest down the back of the *Ceratosaurus* are for show.

This giant can run fast to catch its prey, and has jaws large enough to kill at a single bite.

Ceratosaurus is one of the most common predators in late-Jurassic times, so where there is one, there are likely to be more.

Ceratosaurus is a member of the same family as *Allosaurus* and was at the top of the food chain where it lived.

Meaning of name: Horned lizard
Height: 13 ft (4 m)
Length: 20 ft (6 m)
Family: Ceratosauridae
Period: Late Jurassic
Weight: 1.4 tons (1,300 kg)
Found in: United States
Diet: Meat

The curved claws are well designed for giving deadly blows and for ripping the flesh from a carcass.

IN THE JAWS OF THE GIANTS

▶ Giant meat-eating theropods like *Tyrannosaurus rex* and *Ceratosaurus* have some of the biggest teeth—up to 9 in (23 cm) in length. They are pointed and sharp for tearing flesh and crushing bones.

▼ The largest hadrosaur, *Shantungosaurus*, has at least 378 teeth. Hadrosaurs have the most teeth of any dinosaurs, with rows of up to a thousand very small teeth lined up to chop through tough plants.

▶ Giant sauropods like *Apatosaurus* have small heads and teeth less than 1.6 in (4 cm) long. Their peglike teeth are only useful for biting off leaves to eat.

PLATES AND SPIKES

Taking care not to be spotted, you observe the killer's new prey—a lone *Stegosaurus*. It thrashes its spiked tail and raises its plated back to warn off the predator. Surprisingly, the *Ceratosaurus* wanders off, leaving the *Stegosaurus* to warm its kite-shaped plates in the evening sun. You pitch your tent and eat your one hot meal of the day.

The plates are probably just for show, or to help regulate the dinosaur's body temperature.

The two rows of back plates are too weak to protect the dinosaur from an attack. No one knows for sure what their purpose is.

Stegosaurus has the jaws and teeth to graze and grind. Its cheeks can store food for chewing later.

Stegosaurus is the largest member of the plant-eating family of stegosaurs.

Meaning of name: Roof lizard
Height: 9 ft (2.8 m)
Length: 30 ft (9 m)
Family: Stegosauridae
Period: Late Jurassic
Weight: 3 tons (2,700 kg)
Found in: United States
Diet: Plants

Stegosaurus can swing these fearsome spikes at an approaching predator.

BODY ARMOR

▼ **Saltasaurus** relies on real armor. Its back is covered in small, hornlike bumps, with strong, bony discs under the skin's surface.

▼ **Nodosaurus** is the height of an adult human. Like a tortoise, it can crouch under its bony plates and wait for any predator to tire of trying to break through.

▼ **Wuerhosaurus** has a spiked tail like the *Stegosaurus*, and two rows of back plates too. Stegosaur tails are called "thagomizers." Some bear up to ten deadly spikes.

CALL OF THE DINOSAURS

You are woken by a hornlike alarm. Outside your tent you find a brightly colored beast with a curious crest—a *Parasaurolophus*. It blasts its "horn" again, then a smaller creature comes thundering through the trees. It's a female, attracted to the sound of its mate. However, another creature has also heard the call of the duck-billed dinosaur. These creatures are its favorite prey.

Parasaurolophus is called a duck-billed dinosaur because its beaklike snout is similar to a modern duck's bill.

Meaning of name: Ridged lizard
Height: 9 ft (2.8 m)
Length: 33 ft (10 m)
Family: Hadrosauridae
Period: Late Cretaceous
Weight: 3 tons (2,700 kg)
Found in: Canada, United States
Diet: Plants

The swept back, curved crest, and tail form a streamlined shape that can slip between the undergrowth without being seen.

Tubes in the crest make the hadrosaur's call louder.

The larger crest means that other *Parasaurolophus* recognize it as a male.

A snort from this creature sounds like a blast from a horn or a trombone.

▼ **Corythosaurus** Like the other plant-eating hadrosaurs, *Corythosaurus* has a cutting beak and a mouth crammed with grinding teeth.

▼ **Edmontosaurus** This hadrosaur may inflate its nose to show off. Some scientists think it blows up the loose skin around its nose in the same way a toad blows up a pouch under its chin.

▼ **Lambeosaurus** Like other hadrosaurs, *Lambeosaurus* is a herd dweller. Group living provides safety in numbers, and colorful crests are a useful way of identifying family members.

DEADLY GIANT

Trapped between a *Giganotosaurus* and its prey, you stand frozen with fear. The hungry killer snarls from 36 feet (11 m) above. You nervously admire its clawed fingers, powerful jaw, vicious teeth, and intelligent eyes. It moves slowly, staring at you and the hadrosaurs. It lurches forward, you scream… and then you are saved by a shadow.

Giganotosaurus are the largest known carnivorous dinosaurs.

Unlike *Tyrannosaurus rex*, whose teeth are shaped for crushing and tearing flesh and bone, *Giganotosaurus* has teeth that are flatter and more daggerlike, which work like meat-slicers.

Giganotosaurus is thought to be the largest theropod, but not the biggest dinosaur.

Meaning of name: Giant southern lizard
Height: 10 ft (3 m)
Length: 43 ft (13 m)
Family: Allosauridae
Period: Mid Cretaceous
Weight: 6 tons (5,400 kg)
Found in: Argentina
Diet: Meat

Muscular hind legs and a large tail for balance means *Giganotosaurus* can run fast, in spite of its weight.

BIG AND BRAINY?

A bigger brain in relation to the body of a dinosaur often suggests greater intelligence.

▼ **Tyrannosaurus rex** Although *T. rex* (shown here) has a slightly smaller body than the *Giganotosaurus*, its brain is bigger. Both need large brains as hunting requires intelligence, good eyesight, and speed.

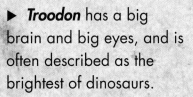

▶ **Troodon** has a big brain and big eyes, and is often described as the brightest of dinosaurs.

▼ **Stegosaurus** This huge creature's brain is the size of a lemon. Some scientists believe it may have another brain elsewhere in its body.

THE GIANT OF GIANTS?

The sky turns black as the dinosaur you've been seeking looms, casting a mountain-sized shadow. You blink, look up, and see the magnificent form of what is probably the biggest dinosaur to have lived—*Argentinosaurus*. The *Giganotosaurus* almost drools at the sight of such a vast meal. Suddenly you are aware of being in the middle of what could be the most violent dinosaur battle ever, so you run for your life.

Colossal sauropods like *Argentinosaurus* need lots of food as they grow into adults. An adolescent probably gains as much as 100 pounds (45 kg) of weight each day.

Argentinosaurus, a sauropod, may be the tallest and heaviest land animal ever to have existed.

Meaning of name: Argentina lizard
Height: 70 ft (21 m)
Length: 120 ft (36 m)
Family: Antarctosauridae
Period: Late Cretaceous
Weight: 121 tons (110,000 kg)
Found in: Argentina
Diet: Plants

Argentinosaurus weighs more than 15 fully-grown elephants put together.

WEIGHING UP THE EVIDENCE

▶ *Argentinosaurus* Little has been found of this dinosaur, but scientists have estimated its size by measuring vertebrae (back bones). Many are 5 ft (1.5 m) tall by 5 ft (1.5 m) wide. That's as tall as an adult human!

▼ *Amphicoelias* will always be a contender for the biggest dinosaur, but the only fossil ever found has been lost—just a drawing exists (see below).

◀ *Seismosaurus* holds the record for being the longest dinosaur, at 131 ft (40 m), because of its impressive tail. However, *Argentinosaurus* was taller and heavier.

CAMOUFLAGE

The sun is setting. It's time to head for the shore, where a boat is due to pick you up and take you home. You wade through the marshes and stop briefly to gaze at familiar markings on unfamiliar creatures. Just as giraffes have camouflage, so do these giant sauropods! You know why they need to hide—you've met some of the terrifying predators they fear.

The *Dicraeosaurus* has an unusually short neck and relatively large head for a sauropod.

As on a giraffe, patches or spots help hide the dinosaur when it is among the shadows of trees.

Dicraeosaurus browse in areas with other plant-eaters, *Giraffatitan* and *Kentrosaurus*. Because each of these is a different height, they eat plants at different levels, so there's no fighting over the juiciest leaves.

Dicraeosaurus is in the same family as **Diplodocus** and has a whiplike tail that is used as a weapon.

Meaning of name: Two forked lizard
Height: 12 ft (3.7 m)
Length: 66 ft (20 m)
Family: Diplodocidae
Period: Late Jurassic
Weight: 6 tons (5,400 kg)
Found in: Tanzania
Diet: Plants

Like all dinosaurs, *Dicraeosaurus* could not swim, but probably waded into rivers for a drink, to cool down, or to escape a passing predator.

COLORFUL DINOSAURS

How do we know about dinosaurs' skin colors and patterns?

▼ **Evidence** Mummified skin tissue from a 67 million-year-old hadrosaur shows that the dinosaur had skin scales of different sizes, suggesting stripes or other patterns. But until we know for sure, artists must use their imagination.

▼ **Camouflage** An armored dinosaur like *Polacanthus* may have had markings that meant they could crouch and hide from predators among the undergrowth.

▶ **Feathers** Fossil evidence shows that many dinosaurs, such as this *Syntarsus*, had feathers for insulation or display.

GIANT SAFARI REPORT

On your way home, you look at the photographs you have taken on your safari. The picture that still makes you shudder is your snap of the *Giganotosaurus*. What could be more terrifying than a giant killer with teeth like sharp knives? And you were within inches of it!

Paleontologists are still trying to work out which of the giants is the size record-holder. New fossils and discoveries are being made all the time, which means a final decision is impossible. Some scientists believe that *Argentinosaurus* is the largest dinosaur ever to have lived. Others argue that *Amphicoelias* or *Bruhathkayosaurus* could have been even bigger (see below). In the future, fossils of even larger monsters may be discovered!

60 m

- Amphicoeliasw
- Bruhathkayosaurus
- Diplodocus
- Supersaurus
- Argentinosaurus
- Brachiosaurus

The incredible inhabitants of your safari location originally lived at two different times during the prehistoric era.

JURASSIC 200 million to 150 million years ago

Stegosaurus

Dicraeosaurus

Brachiosaurus

Apatosaurus

Diplodocus

CRETACEOUS 150 million to 65 million years ago

Giganotosaurus

Ceratosaurus

Parasaurolophus

Spinosaurus

Triceratops

Argentinosaurus

GLOSSARY

camouflage Colorings or markings that make something blend into its setting so that it cannot be seen so easily.

carcass The body of a dead creature.

carrion Flesh from a creature that has died, and a source of food for some animals, such as hyenas.

conifer trees Trees that have needle-shaped leaves and bear cones; examples today are fir and pine trees.

Cretaceous A prehistoric period in which mammals and giant dinosaurs such as *Tyrannosaurus rex* lived. This period ended with the mass extinction of the dinosaurs 65 million years ago.

cycad A type of palm tree that was common in the Jurassic age.

duck-billed dinosaurs Dinosaurs with jaws that are shaped like a duck's bill (beak); also called hadrosaurids.

ellipsoid Oval in shape.

evergreens Plants that have green leaves all year round.

food chain A group of living things that are linked by what eats what; an example of a food chain is a fox eating a rat, and the rat eating an insect, and the insect eating a plant.

fossils Prehistoric remains such as bones or traces such as footprints that have become preserved in rock.

frill A bony area around the neck of a dinosaur.

grazing Feeding on low-growing plants, just as cows feed on grass.

hadrosaurs Plant-eating dinosaurs, also known as duck-billed dinosaurs because of their beaklike mouths.

insulation A way of keeping warm; for example, feathers insulate birds by keeping the warmth in and the cold out.

Jurassic A prehistoric period between 200 and 150 million years ago, during which a huge number of dinosaurs lived.

living fossil A plant or creature that lives today but also lived in prehistoric times in a similar form.

mammals Animals that give birth to live young and feed their young milk. They are warm-blooded.

mummified Preserved in a way that slows down the process of decay. The Egyptians famously mummified their pharaohs, but mummification also happens in nature.

paleontologist A person who studies prehistoric times and evidence such as fossils and rocks.

plates Bony sections on the outer body of a dinosaur that form a kind of armor, or stand up from the spine as on a *Stegosaurus*.

predator An animal that hunts other animals to kill and eat.

prey An animal that is hunted by other animals for food.

reptiles Animals that have scales and cold blood and lay eggs.

sauropod A giant, four-legged, plant-eating dinosaur with a small head but a long neck and tail.

spinosaurids Large two-legged, meat-eating dinosaurs that lived in the Cretaceous period.

streamline The smooth shape of a body or object that helps it move more easily through, for example, woods, water, or the air.

theropods Two-footed, mainly meat-eating dinosaurs such as *Tyrannosaurus rex* and *Giganotosaurus*.

FURTHER READING

Amazing Giant Dinosaurs (DK Children, 2012)

Dinosaur Encyclopedia by Caroline Bingham (Dorling Kindersley, 2009)

Giganotosaurus: The Giant Southern Lizard by Rob Shone (PowerKids Press, 2008)

National Geographic Kids Ultimate Dinopedia: The Most Complete Dinosaur Reference Ever by Don Lessum (National Geographic, 2010)

Princeton Field Guide to Dinosaurs by Gregory S. Paul (Princeton University Press, 2010)

Triceratops Vs Stegosaurus: When Horns and Plates Collide (Dinosaur Wars) by Michael O'Hearn (Raintree, 2011)

WEB SITES

www.amnh.org/exhibitions/fightingdinos/—Information about the American Museum of Natural History's "Fighting Dinosaurs"

http://dsc.discovery.com Discovery Dinosaur Central—search the DinoViewer for size comparisons and how dinosaurs moved

http://ngm.nationalgeographic.com National Geographic—search for the Bizarre Dinosaur section for a closer look at strange dinosaurs

www.nhm.ac.uk/kids-only/dinosaurs/index.html London's Natural History Museum—includes a dinosaur directory and quiz

http://www.jurassicpark.com/site/ Jurassic Park—explore a fictional world of dinosaurs

INDEX